Shaker
Hearts

Shaker Hearts

ANN TURNER

PAINTINGS BY WENDELL MINOR

HARPERCOLLINSPUBLISHERS

The illustrations in this book were painted with acrylics on Masonite panels.

Shaker Hearts
Text copyright © 1997 by Ann Turner
Illustrations copyright © 1997 by Wendell Minor
Printed in the U.S.A. All rights reserved.

Library of Congress Cataloging-in-Publication Data
Turner, Ann Warren.
    Shaker hearts / Ann Turner ; paintings by Wendell Minor.
        p.   cm.
    Summary: Celebrates the way of life of the Shakers who began forming communities in
America in 1774 and who numbered more than 4,000 members in the late 1820s.
    ISBN 0-06-025369-X. — ISBN 0-06-025370-3 (lib. bdg.)
    I. Shakers—United States—Juvenile literature.   [I. Shakers.]   I. Minor, Wendell, ill.   II.
Title.
BX9766.T86   1997   95-45087
284.8—dc20   CIP
                                                                                                                      AC

Typography by Wendell Minor and Al Cetta
1 2 3 4 5 6 7 8 9 10
❖
First Edition

To all the people who run Shaker museums

and make it possible for us to see a part of our past

—A.T.

To the memory of my uncle Andrew Griparis,

a man who understood the simple joys of life.

—W. M.

Author's Note

*I*n 1774, a poor, illiterate Englishwoman called Ann Lee and her eight followers sailed for America and started the Shakers. They were searching for a better life, dedicated to God. They formed their first community near Albany, New York. As time went by, they established over nineteen communities. Some were in New York, Massachusetts, Connecticut, New Hampshire, and Maine. Others were as far away as Kentucky, Ohio, Indiana, and later on even Florida. We believe that by 1823, there were about 4,000 Shakers in America.

The Shakers had their own set of strong beliefs and values. They believed that women and men should not marry or have children together. They lived like monks and nuns in the orderly villages they built. Children came into the communities when orphans were adopted and when new families joined, bringing their children with them. Shaker villages were usually quite neat: As Mother Ann Lee said, "There is no dirt in heaven!" No one could own private property. Throughout much of their history, Shakers gave equal rights to men and women. Black men and women were not discriminated against, and new members had to free their slaves before joining. The Shakers had no ministers or clergy.

They gained the name "Shakers" because of their early practice of dancing wildly and shaking with religious fervor when they worshipped. As time went on, the ecstatic dancing changed, and Shakers added other forms to their worship in inspired paintings, beautiful songs, and spiritual gifts.

Most Shaker communities eventually died out. In the late 1830's people began to leave the Shakers, preferring the freer life in the "world." The rule that men and women could not marry or have children may have been too hard for many. And people were attracted to the growing industries in the "world." Young men and young women left the villages in great numbers.

Shakers are known for their exquisite furniture, designed to be simple and useful. They grew herbs and made medicines. They started the first mail-order seed business, packing seeds in tiny packets with directions on them. They invented many new things, as well as improving older ideas. Shakers are believed to have invented, or patented, an efficient washing machine, the box stove, a revolving oven, and vents to let air into beehives.

There are still a small number of Shakers alive today. Mother Ann predicted that there would be a Shaker revival in the future, and certainly there has been an upwelling of interest in Shakers in recent years. Some of their communities are now museums that you can visit.

It is important to remember that the Shakers ran the most successful utopian communities in America. They influenced the people of their time, and continue to influence us. They gave us an ideal of an ordered and peaceful life dedicated to God. Children were educated, the sick were cared for, and life was lived well and healthfully. That is a gift, indeed.

—A. T.

Bed is neat against the wall,

hands to work, hearts to God,

cloak on wall and shoes on floor

polished in a row.

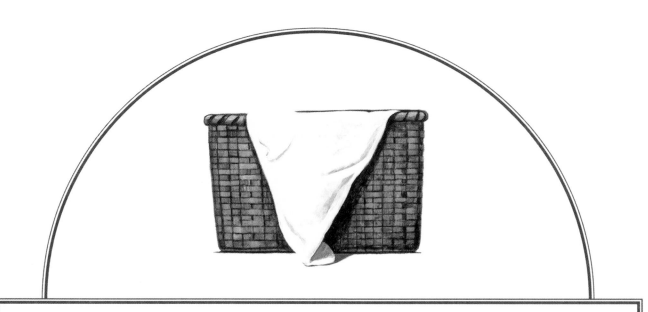

Morning is a golden face,

hands to work, hearts to God,

sisters shake the linens out,

white as morning snow.

Brothers march to sunrise fields,

hands to work, hearts to God,

care for stock and plant the corn,

singing as they sow.

Breakfast on the table lies,

hands to work, hearts to God,

biscuits, pies, and ham and eggs,

let us raise the dough.

Sisters bend to gardens neat,

hands to work, hearts to God,

herbs to knit and mend our bones,

heal them as they grow.

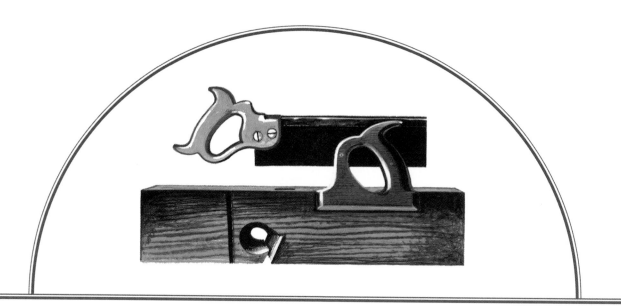

Brothers build the barn go round,

hands to work, hearts to God,

cattle eat the grain and hay,

taken from the mow.

Sisters weave at looms that thump

hands to work, hearts to God,

simple blue and simple black,

lovely row by row.

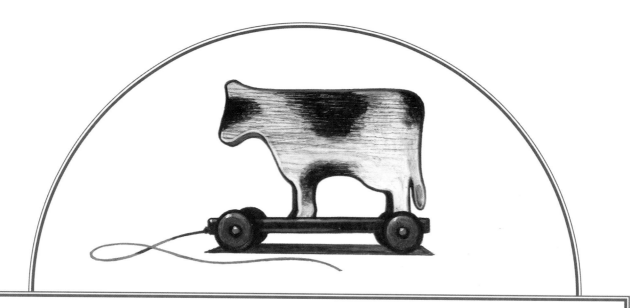

$\mathcal{W}$elcome orphans when they come,

hands to work, hearts to God,

clothe their backs and feed their hearts,

watch them as they grow.

*W*orld moves fast, world moves slow,

hands to work, hearts to God,

put our love in things that work,

hearts and chairs and hoe.

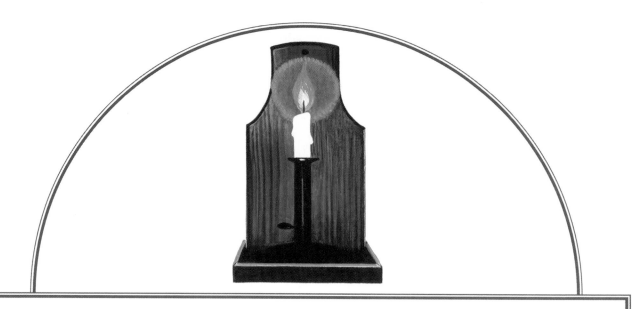

Nighttime comes, dropping down,

hands to work, hearts to God,

meet in blessed shining halls,

singing as we go.

No one knows the love we grow,

hands to work, hearts to God,

like a field of shining grain,

far from world of woe.

Shaker men, Shaker women

equal we are now,

dance our joy with leaping feet,

loving as we go.

HANDS
TO WORK,
HEARTS
TO GOD.

—Mother Ann Lee

The Shakers are known for their fine inventions and improvements on earlier ones. They strove for the best and most efficient way in everything—from washing clothes and shelling peas to packaging seeds and feeding cows. But they are also known for their forward-looking practices, which included giving equal rights to freed slaves and providing a good education for their children.

PEGS ON THE WALL: Shakers hung their chairs on wall pegs so the rooms would be easy to clean. Clean and neat houses, yards, and work buildings were a mark of Shaker communities and may have contributed to the Shakers' longevity.

THE ROUND BARN: Although it is the only one built by the Shakers, the round barn at Hancock Village, Massachusetts, fits in with Shaker beliefs and philosophy. One man could fork out enough hay to feed a whole herd of cows gathered around. Because the barn was so efficient, people could spend less time feeding cows and more time worshipping God.

HERB GARDENS: While not the first people to practice herbal medicine, the Shakers perfected it. They grew great quantities of herbs, dried them in a special vacuum extractor of their own invention, and manufactured oils, powders, and pills. They used them to help treat various diseases among the Shakers as well as the "world's" people.

SEED PACKETS: The Shakers invented small paper packets to hold seeds for planting. These included instructions for planting the seeds and, in later years, colored pictures of the vegetables. Many pioneers going west owed the success of their gardens partly to the Shakers' high-quality seeds and good instructions. As with all Shaker products, people could count on their excellence.

SHAKER FOOD: In an age when most people's diets were heavy with meat, salt, alcohol, and caffeine, the Shakers were known for their diet of hearty, healthy food. Some communities forbade caffeine and alcohol, and also tried a vegetarian diet for a while. The Shakers included grains, vegetables, and fruits along with meats and breads. Their home-grown herbs added special flavor to their meals.

LIGHT: The Shakers used great quantities of windows in their buildings, even in their barns. They delighted in natural light, using skylights in their attics. This reduced the need for candles and lanterns, thus lowering the danger of fires.

DANCING: In the early years, the Shakers were known for their "shaking" dancing, which was part of their worship of God. Over the years, the dancing became calmer and more organized, sometimes moving in circles (men going one way, women the other), or in lines. Dancing was meant to bring the Shakers closer to God.

CHILDREN: The Shakers loved children and took great care over their upbringing and education. Some from the "world" sent their children to the superior Shaker schools, where they, too, could learn reading, writing, arithmetic, geography, and in some cases astronomy and botany.

EQUALITY: The Shakers were unique in giving women an important role in running their communities. They were far ahead of their time in forbidding new members to bring slaves into their villages. Shakers even bought the freedom of some slaves so that they could join their communities as equal members.

Date Due

OCT 24 1988					